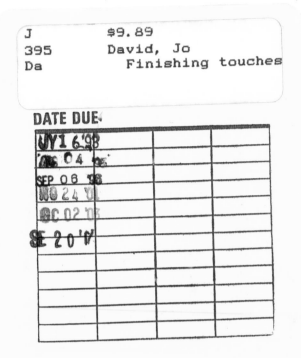

Finishing Touches

SMART TALK

Finishing Touches:
Manners with Style

Jo David

Troll Associates

Library of Congress Cataloging-in-Publication Data

David, Jo.
    Finishing touches: manners with style / by Jo David; illustrated
by Donald Richey.
        p.   cm.—(Smart talk)
    Summary: Guidelines for courteous behavior in every situation.
    ISBN 0-8167-2179-3 (lib. bdg.)   ISBN 0-8167-2180-7 (pbk.)
    1. Etiquette for children and teenagers.   2. Etiquette—United
States—Juvenile literature.   [1. Etiquette.]   I. Richey, Donald,
ill.   II. Title.   III. Series.
BJ1857.C5D28   1991
395'.123—dc20   90-10888

Table of Contents

Act Like a Lady? Give Me a Break!

"**W**hen I grow up, I'll be able to do whatever I want." Does this sound familiar? When you were younger and wanted to do something your parents wouldn't let you do, did you think it to yourself? It probably seemed like growing up was a

1

guarantee of total freedom— you could do whatever you wanted to do.

And then, all of a sudden, you may have realized that getting older also means taking more responsibility for yourself and for other people! And you realized that other people's feelings count as much as your own. It isn't easy to figure out what people expect of you. And constantly being told to "mind your manners" makes it seem as though the world is full of traps just waiting to snare you.

The truth is, good manners aren't supposed to test you or trip you up. In fact, manners make life a whole lot easier! They can be tricky at first, but eventually you'll find that good manners will become second nature. And you'll see that they make you more comfortable with yourself and everyone around you—your parents, your friends, your classmates . . . even your teachers!

There are three things that describe what manners are really all about: common sense, compromise and caring. As long as you understand these three and know how to use them, any social or personal relationships you have will be a lot easier. And you can use them forever, not just in junior high or high school. The places you go and people you meet will change as you grow older, but the basic concepts of courtesy remain constant.

When you're growing up, it may seem like a lot of work to figure out what's courteous and what's not. This book will show you everything you need to know, not just the basic "do's and don'ts" of how to be polite. Remember: Being polite is about being *you*, so don't try to be phony. If you act politely, pretty soon it will become natural. Being a courteous person makes it fun to be nice to people—and makes *you* more fun to be around!

MODERN MANNERS FOR TODAY'S TEENS

Once upon a time, "manners" meant something very different from what it does today. For example: More recently than you may believe, a woman never left home without wearing a hat and gloves. These weren't really manners, however. They were simply customs—behavior that was socially acceptable at that period in time. Today, people would think you were crazy if you went around curtsying to everyone you met. But at one time, that's just the way things were done. And a big part of having good manners is respecting the customs of the day or of the place you live.

Lots of people confuse customs with manners, or think that such things as knowing which fork to use automatically make a person appear more "cultured" or mannerly. The fact of the matter is, *good manners are just good sense.* If you treat others as you would like them to treat you, that's courtesy! It's as simple as that.

As times have changed, many customs have become less formal than they were in the past—but in a way, that makes the maze of manners even more confusing! You may feel like you'll never learn what's right and what's wrong. But don't give up. It all depends on how you look at it.

The truth is, manners aren't really rules. They're *guidelines* for how to behave in every situation, whether you're at school, at home or traveling around the world. All you have to remember is to use your common sense, think before you speak and always, *always* consider other people's feelings. Courtesy isn't about being "right" or "correct." It's a way to make others feel comfortable—and to make you feel good about yourself, too. And a considerate person is a popular person.

What does it mean to "mind your manners?" Does being polite mean you can never be yourself and you have to be nice to everyone, no matter what? Try our courtesy quiz and find out!

For all quizzes, please write your answers on a separate sheet of paper.

4

☆☆ **COURTESY QUIZ** ☆☆

1. *You should curtsy when introduced to an adult at a formal function.*
   True or False

2. *Once you've grown up, you have to sit quietly at outdoor parties while the guys are having fun in the backyard.*
   True or False

3. *If you wear white gloves when you go to a restaurant or theater, it shows you have good manners.*
   True or False

4. *It's polite to let every relative in the world kiss you at a family reunion, whether you know them or not.*
   True or False

5. *If you use the wrong fork at dinner, everyone will know you're impolite.*
   True or False

6. *If you say "please" and "thank you" all the time, without really meaning it, you are being polite.*
   True or False

Hopefully, you won't be surprised that the answer to all these questions is **FALSE**! And if you thought the answers to more than three of these were true, wake up! This isn't the Victorian Age!

So how does all this work in real life? Read on!

The Politeness Puzzle

*T*here are ten pieces in the politeness puzzle. In other words, there are basically ten things you need to do to be a polite person. Learning how and when to use them is a snap! And then, the rest is just common sense.

6

The Ten "Polite" Pieces

1. Say "please" and "thank you" for every-thing—and mean it.

2. Try not to interrupt when someone else is talking.

3. Say "excuse me" if you absolutely *have to* interrupt someone, leave the table or the room or slide past someone who is in your way.

4. Smile and shake hands when you're intro-duced to someone. Try to remember that person's name.

5. Answer the phone pleasantly.

6. Write thank-you notes promptly for gifts and whenever you're a house guest or the recipi-ent of some special attention.

7. Look at people when they're talking to you. Try to take an interest in what they're saying.

8. Always use good table manners.

9. Accept compliments gracefully.

10. Remember that other peoples' needs and feel-ings are as important as your own.

PIECE ONE—Say "Please" and "Thank You" for Everything—and Mean It

Saying "please" and "thank you" is the *key* to the politeness puzzle. If in doubt, say the magic words. You might feel like you're saying it for everything, but this is one case where you can never really overdo it. But, be sure you *mean* it.

You can't just go through the motions of good manners. Saying "please" is the right thing to do, but if you say "Please pass the potatoes" and then gobble up the whole bowl, you've blown it. Or, what if you always say "thank you" to strangers, but gossip about your friends? Merely parroting the words won't help anyone!

PIECE TWO—Try Not to Interrupt When Someone Else Is Talking

It is really bad manners to interrupt people. The only exception is if you've got the kind of family where everybody talks at once at the dinner table and interrupting is the only way to get a word in edgewise! In families such as this, a certain amount of interruption is acceptable as a survival tactic. But always interrupt politely and excuse yourself, and by no means should you interrupt in other places, or if you have company at home.

PIECE THREE—Say "Excuse Me" if You Absolutely Have to Interrupt Someone, Leave the Table or the Room or Slide Past Someone Who Is in Your Way

This is another all–purpose expression that is good for almost any situation where you do not want to appear rude. When in doubt, excuse yourself—it can never hurt.

PIECE FOUR—Smile and Shake Hands When You're Introduced to Someone, and Try to Remember That Person's Name

We all know that curtsying went out with the horse-drawn carriage. But what is the proper way to greet people nowadays? With your friends and family, a simple "Hi" may seem just fine, but what happens when you meet someone new?

The most foolproof greeting is also the most simple. When you're introduced to someone, shake hands, smile and say "Hello." And make sure it's a nice, firm handshake, not one of those clammy, shaky kinds that give you the creeps! Believe it or not, having a good handshake is really important. That's because the way you shake hands says a lot about you.

Let your handshake tell people that you are someone they want to get to know.

What Does Your Handshake Say About You? An Easy Guide to the Perfect Handshake—and What Not to Do!

Type	Description	What It Says About You
"Fearful Flora"	Grasp the person's fingertips with your fingertips. Do not apply any pressure and drop the other person's fingers as soon as possible. Skin feels dry and cool.	You are afraid of getting involved with people and you wish to limit the amount of contact you have with them.
"Dead Fish Phyllis"	Place your hand in the other person's hand, but don't really grasp it. Don't apply any pressure and don't shake at all. Skin feels sweaty.	You are anxious about meeting people. You don't want too much contact and you really wish that people would leave you alone.

11

"Strong-Arm Sally"	Grasp the other person's hand with your whole hand and squeeze as hard as you can, preventing the other person from squeezing back. Keep arm stiff, no shaking at all.	You are very insecure and afraid that others will perceive you as weak. You feel a need to show that no one can push you around and that you can control any situation.
"Honest Abby"	Firmly grasp the person's hand with your whole hand. Apply gentle pressure and shake it once or twice. (Note: You always shake hands with your right hand.) Your skin feels dry and warm to the touch.	You are sincere, friendly and honest—someone people like to be with.

Handshakes say a lot, but there are other ways of greeting people, too. Some people give their friends big hugs whenever they see them. And what about kissing? Naturally, you can't go around kissing everyone you meet, but on occasion, and especially with relatives, giving someone a kiss on the cheek is a nice thing to do.

Meeting new people can be very confusing, especially at a party where you might meet several people at once. Always smile and greet people warmly. And it's key to remember the person's name. If you didn't hear it, or didn't understand it, ask the person to repeat it.

Remembering names can be difficult. Fortunately, there are some tricks that can help. One method is to look at the person's face and repeat his or her name to yourself three or four times. Some experts suggest trying word association, too. For instance, if you met someone named Alice who had rosy cheeks, you might think, Alice Apple. The connection doesn't have to make sense, but it's surprising how well it works!

If you do forget a person's name, though, it's not the end of the world. If it happens, you should say something like, "I know we've been introduced, but I've met so many new people today. Please tell me your name again." When the person tells you, repeat it out loud, smile and say, "Thank you. I'll try to remember."

PIECE FIVE—Answer the Phone Pleasantly

The correct way to answer a phone is to say, "Hello" or "Smith residence" (provided, of course, your name is Smith). Saying "Yeah?" or demanding "Who is this?" are both definitely impolite.

The same goes for calling someone else. Never demand, "Is Patty there?" or mumble, "Lemme talk to Patty." Instead, say with a pleasant voice, "Hello. This is Holly Carson. May I speak to Patty, please?" If you know the person who answers, you can say, "Hello, Mrs. Abramson, this is Holly. May I speak to Patty, please?" The person you call has every right to know who is at the other end of the line—just as it is perfectly correct for you to say, "May I ask who is calling?" or "May I tell Peter who is calling?" when someone calls your house.

Besides answering the phone, there are some other very important elements of phone etiquette. Never tie up the line for long periods of time, especially if other people in the house want to use the phone. This goes double if you know that someone in your house is expecting a call; in that case, don't use the phone without first asking the person waiting for the call if it is all right with him or her. If someone calls you, politely explain that you'd love to talk, but your sister is waiting for a call and you can't tie up the line. Tell your friends you'll call them back as soon as you can.

When taking messages for others it is extremely important to remember your manners. Always write down the name of the caller, along with the date and time of the call. Don't hesitate to ask the person to spell his or her name if you didn't get it the first time. Remember to ask for a number where the caller can be reached. You shouldn't feel obligated to give the caller information about where the person he or she called is or when that person will be back, and so on. In fact, if you don't know the person, you should give them as little information as possible.

Finally, never, *ever* listen in on someone else's call. This is not only rude, it's a lot easier to get caught than you may think it is! And just imagine how you'd feel if someone listened in on your calls!

PIECE SIX—Write Thank-You Notes Promptly for Gifts and Whenever You're a House Guest or the Recipient of Some Special Attention

This is one of the most important pieces of the politeness puzzle and, unfortunately, one of the most neglected. Maybe this is because it can be hard to know what to say in a thank-you note. Let's face it! How many times can you write "Thank you for the lovely gift. I'll really enjoy using it" before you go insane? It's a lot more fun to write a creative thank-you note. Just make sure you include the basics. Take a look at the examples below.

★★★

Thank-You Note DO's

1. DO mention the specific gift. For example:
   –"Thank you for the lovely sweater."

–"Thank you for taking me to the ballet."
–"Thank you for having me to your home this weekend."
–"Thank you for asking me to dinner the other night."

2. DO mention something that is special to you about the gift or the special treat you were given. For example:
   –"Blue is my favorite color."
   –"I have always wanted to see 'Swan Lake.'"
   –"It's such a treat to have a weekend in the country."
   –"I always enjoy spending time with your family."

3. DO say something that shows the gift or treat will have continuing importance to you. For example:
   –"I look forward to wearing the beautiful sweater you gave me."
   –"I will remember the performance for a long time."
   –"I will remember the fun we had for a long time."

4. DO say something to indicate that you look forward to returning the person's generosity.
   –"I hope I can find as wonderful a gift for your birthday."
   –"I hope to return your hospitality in the city very soon."
   –"I hope you can join my family for dinner soon."

5. DO say thank you. Although you don't have to start the letter by saying "Thank you," you should say it at least once. Twice is even better.

6. DO write the note on the day the present is received, if possible, or else the very next day. One of the main purposes of thank-you notes is to tell the person that you received the gift, so sending the note a month later doesn't help very much. It's also easier to remember if you do it on the same day.

7. DO write the note on your own stationery or on a pretty note card. The note must be neat and all the words in the note should be spelled correctly, especially the person's name. Use a dictionary if you're not sure or ask your parents. Making everything "just right" shows your appreciation for the gift.

8. DO write the note out on a blank sheet of paper first and show it to one of your parents. They can be helpful in correcting spelling errors and grammar. Then copy your note neatly onto your stationery or the note card.

9. DO sign your letter "Sincerely," or "Love," depending on your relationship with the giver.

Thank-You Note DON'Ts

1. DON'T mention that you already have the same or a similar gift, or say that you had to, or wished to, return the gift.

2. DON'T say anything negative about the gift (for example, it didn't fit or you didn't really care for the ballet).

3. DON'T start your note by apologizing. If your note is late, explain why *after* you thank the person for a gift.

4. DON'T type a thank-you note. Always write it by hand.

Note: If you are sending thank-you notes to several people who know each other and might have the opportunity to compare or discuss the notes, be careful to individualize the notes, so that it doesn't look like you used the same note for all of them and just changed the names!

★★★

We're not saying that you have to write a thank-you note for every single gift you receive. Certainly you don't have to send one to your mother or to your best friend whom you see every day at school. If someone you see quite often hands you a gift, simply thank them. If they send you a gift you should call to enthusiastically acknowledge it. But for those instances where a thank-you note is appropriate, a well-written note is vital.

PIECE SEVEN—Look at People When They're Talking to You. Try to Take an Interest in What They're Saying

Dear Smart Talk,

The other day at school I was sitting in the cafeteria with my friend Ginny. But while I was trying to talk to her, she was looking around the cafeteria and not paying attention to a word I was saying. Then, she got up without saying anything and went over to another table to talk to a boy we know. Even though she came back to finish her lunch, I was so upset I couldn't finish the conversation. I thought Ginny was really rude, but when I told another friend about it later, she said there was nothing wrong with the way Ginny acted— that she was just being sociable. What do you think?

Carolyn

Dear Carolyn,

Ginny was very rude. Even if she had something very important to say to someone else and it couldn't wait until later, she should have at least excused herself, explained why she was getting up and apologized when she came back. At a dinner or a party, or anywhere, it is wrong to ignore the person you're with. Having a "swivel neck" is just plain rude.

19

That doesn't mean, though, that you should totally ignore everyone around you. At a dinner party, for instance, polite guests talk to the people seated on either side of them, as well as the person opposite them. It is not polite to ignore anyone, and it is not polite to monopolize one person's attention.

PIECE EIGHT—*Always Use Good Table Manners*

It's not just that people with good table manners are polite—it's that people without them are disgusting! How would you like to sit across from someone who chews with their mouth open or talks through a mouthful of food? Yech!

Even if you're eating at home or by yourself, you should use good table manners because it's easy—though not excusable!—to get lazy. So, use them all the time and before long, they'll be second nature and you won't even have to think about them.

Here are the most important ones:

Table Manners

✪ *Don't chew with your mouth open.*

✪ *Never talk with your mouth full.*

✪ *Don't rest your elbows on the table while eating.*

✪ *Always ask for things to be passed—never reach across the table to grab something.*

✪ *Don't start eating until everyone else has been served, unless specifically told otherwise by your host or hostess.*

✪ *Keep your napkin on your lap—not only is this good manners, but it's also a good idea in case you happen to spill something!*

✪ *If you need to leave the table, always ask to be excused—don't just get up and go.*

✪ *No food fights! There is nothing more disgusting or rude—not to mention the fact that it's a waste of good food.*

✪ *Don't complain about what's being served. If you don't like something, don't eat it, but don't call attention to it, either—that's insulting to the host or hostess. Also, other people may be enjoying it.*

One more thing—don't forget that these tips apply to eating *everywhere*, whether it's at school, at home or in a restaurant.

PIECE NINE—Accept Compliments Gracefully

A compliment is one of the nicest things someone can give you. But do you know how to react to one? A lot of people become embarrassed by compliments and so they don't know what to say or how to act. The answer is simple: Just smile and say "thank you." Really, that's all you have to do. People don't say nice things to you for any reward. They just want to make you feel good. In fact, if you say too much you can make them feel foolish. The same goes for giving compliments. Always phrase them carefully.

Here are some common goofs made in both receiving and giving compliments:

Situation	You Say	Problem
Your friend says, "Mary, what a terrific sweater!"	"What, this ugly thing?"	You've just insulted your friend's taste. Even if you hate your clothes or think your new haircut is a disaster, thank the person anyway. Maybe it's not as bad as you believe.

You see a friend who's been away all summer and has lost a good deal of weight.	"Wow! You've lost a ton!"	This isn't really a compliment—it's an insult to the way she looked before. You should say, "Mandy, you look terrific!" If she's really lost a remarkable amount of weight, she'll probably appreciate you noticing her efforts. Say something like, "You really look super. You must feel good about slimming down." Rather than reminding her of her previous appearance, this reinforces her pride in her accomplishment.
Someone tells you, "Your eyes are really pretty."	Embarrassed, you say, "Aw, no they're not."	Never contradict a compliment. The person wouldn't have said it if they didn't mean it.
You're at a party where everyone is dressed up.	To one girl in a large group, "What a fabulous dress."	You should never slight others by singling out only one person to compliment. If you want to compliment everyone, say something like, "You

all look so pretty!" If you want to give a special compliment to a close friend or you truly adore someone's dress, hair style, etc., do it later when you are not in a group.

Sometimes, people give backhanded compliments. This is praise that isn't actually very flattering, or maybe just not phrased very well. For instance, someone might say, "Boy, I never realized you were so smart!" You're wondering, "Why not? Do I look dumb?" But avoid giving sarcastic answers. Instead say, "Thank you. I studied hard for this test."

Here are a few more tips on compliments: *Be creative.* Saying, "That shade of blue really brings out your eyes" is a lot more meaningful than "I like your blouse."

Never fish for compliments. Avoid phrases like, "Don't you like my new skirt?" If your friends hate it, you're putting them in a position where they'll either have to lie or hurt your feelings. Likewise, if someone asks you for your opinion, *use your best judgment.* You should always try to be honest, but there's nothing polite about hurting someone's feelings. If you really don't like their cooking or their new haircut, try to find *something* positive to say.

Always be sincere. And don't overuse compliments. If you compliment everyone all the time, your words of praise will lose their meaning.

PIECE TEN—*Remember That Other People's Needs and Feelings Are as Important as Your Own*

Who is a true friend? Someone who is always talking about herself, or someone who calls you and asks you how *you* are—and really wants to know? Even if she has a problem and really wants to talk to you about it, she takes the time to ask about you first. That's what courtesy is all about.

Sometimes it's not easy to think about other people's feelings, especially if you're upset, but if you care about someone, you should make an effort to do it at all times. Remember, someday you'll need them to be there for you, and you can't expect to be treated well if you don't show the same consideration to others. That's why manners are so important. A lot of the things that are considered polite are really things that protect other people's feelings from being hurt.

Now that you've got all the pieces, you're prepared for almost anything. The tricky part is learning how to put the pieces together in various situations. Read on!

Courtesy Begins at Home

*L*eigh is always mindful of her manners. She is considerate to her friends and teachers, and helpful to strangers. When she eats dinner or stays overnight at a friend's house, her friend's parents always remark on Leigh's courtesy and warmly invite her to come back as often as she wishes.

But at home, Leigh is different. She is often sulky with her parents and is constantly arguing with her brothers. As soon as she finishes eating she leaves the table and disappears into her room for the rest of the evening.

Does Leigh have good manners? Absolutely not!

Courtesy doesn't stop the minute you walk through your own front door. In fact, your family deserves as much consideration as other people—if not more. Just because you see them every day doesn't excuse you from being polite. Still, the sad truth is that a lot of teens and pre-teens who go out of the way to be kind and thoughtful to others seem to act as though their families just aren't very important when it comes to manners.

Sometimes it's hard to remember those puzzle pieces and be courteous to your family. After all, they know you, so why do you have to be polite when you've had a lousy day and just want to be by yourself? Of course, manners are more relaxed at home. But even when you're annoyed with your parents or just dying to strangle your kid brother, remember that every member of your family has feelings, too. Besides, when good manners become a habit at home, they're easier to remember when you're someplace else.

PARENT POINTERS

This may be a difficult time for you, especially when it comes to getting along with your parents. You want to cut loose and get out on your own, choose your own friends and clothes and not have to answer a lot of questions. Your parents, on the other hand, are just as concerned about you as they were when you were a little kid. They may be reluctant to give you the freedom you want at first (especially if you are the oldest child). You may also be more sensitive to their criticism at this time. But this doesn't have to mean the end of a civil relationship with your parents! In fact, the more mature and cooperative you are about settling your differences, the more willing they'll be to see your point of view. Here are some tips to help you be polite to your parents:

Never talk back to your parents—it's counterproductive. Being snotty will just make them think of you as a kid, and that's the last thing you want! If they ask you a question, answer it. Never, never snap, "It's none of your business!" or mumble something vague. Your parents have a *right* to be concerned about you. Keep your cool even if you think they're just being nosy. Calmly tell them that you know they're trying to be helpful, but you feel that this is a private area. Assure them that if you need their advice you will ask for it.

Be helpful at home. If your parents ask you to do chores, do them without grumbling or complaining. Don't forget that your parents are busy people, too. Is it fair for them to have to do *everything?*

Respect your parents' rules. If they don't want the phone ringing after a certain hour, make sure you let your friends know when they can call. If you have a curfew, don't break it! The way to get your parents to realize that you're growing up is to demonstrate that you are a responsible person.

If your parents don't set rigid rules, use your common sense and respect their feelings. Even if your mother never tells you when you need to be home or doesn't ask you to call her when you arrive somewhere, you can bet she's still worrying about you. If you think you're going to be late, pick up the phone! You'll feel a lot better—and so will your parents.

Never invite anyone to your house without checking with your parents first. It may be the night your mom's boss is coming to dinner, or there may be nothing but leftovers in the fridge. Your parents may be planning to go out or to have their own friends over. Or the house may be a mess! Always offer to pitch in if you have friends coming over. It's not your mom or dad's responsibility to have a spotless house and a stocked refrigerator waiting. If you are planning to invite a friend to dinner, for example, talk it over with your parents first, and then offer to do more than your usual share of kitchen tasks. Your parents will appreciate it, and will probably be more open to your having guests in the future.

By the same token, if you're planning to have dinner at a friend's, or to spend the night, give your parents as much notice as possible. Don't call your mother at five minutes to six, when she's about to take your dinner out of the oven, and tell her you won't be there to eat it. That's just not nice. And, if your parents were hoping you could baby-sit your little sister on a night you've been invited to a slumber party, giving them lots of notice will allow them to make other plans. That way you won't be stuck staying home just because it was too late to make other arrangements!

Finally, **respect your parents' privacy**. Even if they're having an argument, don't get involved. That's something between the two of them, and interfering never helps.

It might be hard for your parents to find time to spend together without the kids. Maybe you and your brothers and sisters could volunteer to fix your own dinners one night a week so that they can go out. Your parents will appreciate it, and if you behave yourselves well they'll probably be willing to leave you alone more often.

Being considerate to your parents is just like being considerate to anyone else. All it takes is some practice, and you'll be amazed at the results!

SURVIVING SIBLINGS

You're probably thinking, how can I possibly be polite to my obnoxious brother who is always getting into my things, listening in on my phone conversations and making fun of all my friends? The slime doesn't deserve it!

Maybe not, but you should do it anyway. The good thing about brothers is that they usually grow up to be nice guys, and sometimes they even have cute friends. Aside from that, though, they can be pretty difficult people to have around sometimes. Sisters are about the same. While they may not put rubber spiders in your bed, they can be bossy or bratty. And little sisters can be a big pain in the neck—especially if your parents expect you to drag them with you everywhere you go. It's probably at times like these that you find yourself wishing with all your heart that you were an only child. But even when you think your siblings ought to be sent off on a rocket ship to Mars so you can have some peace on Earth, you have to remember that, like it or not, you're stuck with them.

But seriously, you don't despise your brothers and sisters all the time, do you? Sometimes they can actually be pretty good to have around. Older siblings can be a great source of advice, and younger siblings will always look up to you as an older sister—that can be a pretty special feeling, when you think about it.

Sharing the good times with your sister will make them even better!

The golden rule of manners among siblings is this: *Respect their privacy as you would have them respect yours*. The number one cause of sibling rivalry is the fact that you are always in each other's way! You can't expect your sister to stay out of your bureau if you don't stay out of her closet. It's extremely rude to pry into someone else's stuff, or to use something that belongs to someone else without asking. When you're all living in the same house, it can be hard to remember this. But manners are manners, no matter how well you know a person. Which means even if you're sure your sister won't mind if you borrow her favorite blouse, ask her anyway!

If you have to share a room, a little advance planning can make life much easier in the long run. Talk with your sister about how you will divide the space in the closet, and so on. If there are times you'd like to be alone, or have friends over, let your sister know when that's likely to be. And respect her privacy, too. Don't have your friends up to listen to records while she's trying to study for a test.

Try to keep your things as neat as possible. This is true even if you have your own room, but it's absolutely *essential* if you're sharing. If your sister's a slob, ask her politely to clean her half of the room. If you share a bathroom with your sisters or brothers, keep that neat, too. And try not to take half-hour-long showers, especially in the mornings when you're all trying to rush out and get to school.

No matter what you do, when you have a disagreement with a sibling try to work things out between yourselves before going to your parents. Your sister won't like you any better for getting your parents involved and maybe getting you *both* in trouble. Your parents will probably think you're acting like children—and you know what that can lead to!

GENERAL FAMILY COURTESY

You should stick up for your family. You're a unit and, good or bad, they reflect on you and vice versa. They're a part of you—a part you should always be proud of.

Try to avoid talking with friends—or anyone—about private family matters. These include such things as finances, problems that could be embarrassing to your family or other personal matters. These things are nobody else's business. If people ask you insensitive questions such as, "How much money does your family have?" or "Do your parents fight a lot?" the correct answer is always, "I'm sorry, but I feel that's a personal matter." If they continue to pester you, keep saying it until they get the point.

Dear Smart Talk,

My little brother Greg is a year behind me in school, even though he's about ten times smarter than I am. The problem is, a lot of the "cool" kids in school think he's a real geek. I want to fit in with the right crowd, but I think my brother's great and no matter what, I can't ignore him in the halls just to be popular. What should I do?

Candi

Dear Candi:

You're on the right track! Never act like you're ashamed of your family. What would it say about you if you couldn't even be nice to your own brother? And don't worry, people won't say, "Candi's nice except for her weird brother." Instead they'll say, "Any guy with a sister as nice as Candi must be okay." Believe it!

AVOIDING ARGUMENTS

Arguments happen sometimes in all families. They're never fun, but good manners can really make them easier. Some people have the strange idea that good manners mean you have to agree with everything everyone else says and, therefore, by the time you're arguing, it's already too late for manners. This couldn't be further from the truth! Whether or not you disagree with someone has nothing to do with being polite. But there is an art to disagreeing with people. How you do it is where manners come in.

For instance, calling someone a name or saying, "Oh, come on, do you really believe that?" is definitely out. Not only is it rude, it shows people that you don't know how to make your own point. Putting people down is just as bad. And don't forget, everyone has the right to his or her own opinion. Respect that right!

★★★

Discussion DO's

1. DO think about what you want to say before you say it.

2. DO make your argument point by point.

3. DO keep "a smile" in your voice.

4. DO decide which things are most important to argue about.

5. DO use facts and figures to support your point of view.

6. DO conclude the disagreement on a friendly note, if possible.

Discussion DON'Ts

1. DON'T say the first thing that comes to mind.

2. DON'T say "I just know I'm right."

3. DON'T raise your voice, or sound defensive.

4. DON'T argue with everybody about everything.

5. DON'T generalize and say things like "Every-body knows it's true."

6. DON'T let a family relationship be ruined over a disagreement.

★★★

Your family is an important part of your life—they're the people you'll have to be around for longer than anyone. Don't they deserve the best you can give?

Adults Are People, Too!

*O*ne of the most important things good manners can do is to help you get along better with people. Being with your friends is easy—you're the same age and share many of the same ideas and experiences. That's why you're friends! But with adults, it can be much more difficult to know what's expected of you. You don't have as much in common, so you may find it harder to be with them. Like it or not, though, part of growing up is learning how to deal with all types of people, of every age. The good news is, the rules are about the same.

For starters: If you want to be treated like an adult, act like one! If you treat others courteously and remember the puzzle pieces, you'll find that adults are far more likely to treat you as an equal and take you seriously.

TALKING TO ADULTS

One of the most perplexing problems when it comes to dealing with adults is making conversation. This is especially true with adults you don't know very well, such as relatives you don't see often, or your parents' friends. Relax! The generation gap is not as wide as you may think it is. Don't forget that every adult was once your age.

Try not to answer questions with a simple yes or no. That is the number one conversation killer! If someone asks you a yes or no question, salvage the situation by volunteering more information.

For example, if your aunt asks you whether you play a musical instrument, don't just say, "Yes," or even worse, "Yeah." Say, "Yes, I'm learning the clarinet. I like it a lot." Or, even better, "Yes, I play the clarinet. Do you play an instrument?" That gives the ball back to her and she can continue the conversation. You may even find you have something in common!

You can't expect the adult to be the one to start talking every time, though. Sitting in silence has not been considered good manners since the bad old days when children were seen and not heard. If you are with some adults and there is an uncomfortable silence in the room, it's polite to strike up a conversation. This might seem like an impossible task, but it's really quite easy. Here are some good ideas for things to talk about:

Jobs. Ask them if they have a job, and what it is. Ask them what they like about it, or if it's what they wanted to do when they were younger.

Connections. If they're friends of your parents, ask them how they met your parents. This can be interesting, especially if they're old friends—you may learn a lot about what your parents were like when they were younger.

Interests. Ask them about hobbies, or places they may have traveled to. If they're from out of town, ask them how they like your town and what it's like in their part of the country (or the world).

Yourself. If you can't think of anything to ask about them, try telling them something about yourself that might be a good topic of conversation. For example, tell them about a vacation you took recently, and then ask about their last vacation.

With a little effort and some practice, you should find that adults aren't that difficult to talk to after all.

HELP THEM SEE THE REAL YOU

You may feel that many people, especially relatives who've known you all your life, will insist on treating you like a child. This can be very aggravating. Here is an example. How would you deal with this situation?

Your grandmother gives you a nightgown that has cartoon animals all over it. You would have loved it a few years ago, but now you wouldn't be caught dead wearing it! Which is the correct response?

a) "Ugh, this is for babies. Don't you know I'm not a little kid anymore?"

b) "Grandma, this is really cute, but I feel I'm a little too grown-up for this style. I really appreciate the thought, but would you mind if I exchanged it?"

c) "Thank you, Grandma! This is so nice of you."

Obviously, A is downright rude. Not only is it ungrateful, and an insult to your grandmother's taste, but you're also putting your grandmother down in a very unkind way. Answer B may seem like a mature thing to do, but it is still impolite to criticize a gift just after receiving it.

Answer C is the best, but after you thank your grandmother (and write her a thank-you note, if appropriate) you should talk to your mother about how your tastes have changed. Maybe she can tactfully bring up the subject with your grandmother before she goes shopping for your next birthday! That way you'll get something you like, and she won't waste her money.

HANDLE WITH CARE

Finally, here are a few special manners to keep in mind when dealing with adults:

Always be respectful. Unless an adult is being abusive or downright disgusting, remember that they are older than you are and, as such, deserve respect. Don't talk back or complain when they ask you to do something.

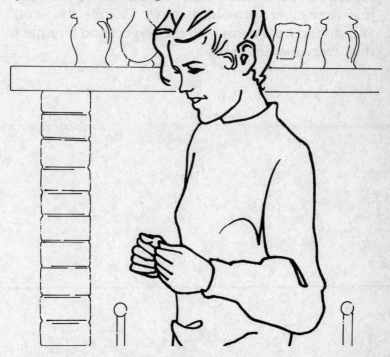

Talking to older adults will enrich their lives—and yours.

Be aware of the special needs of older people, especially elderly people. Your grandfather may need to take a nap in the afternoon. Be quiet and let him sleep! If you have elderly relatives or friends who have trouble getting around or who are ill, offer to help them with chores, or getting up the stairs. But always ask first! Don't just barge in and try to help. They may be sensitive and may resent being treated like invalids (kind of the same way you resent being treated like a baby!).

Learning to live with the adults in your life may sometimes be difficult, but it can also be rewarding. Just remember, grownups have feelings too, and you should treat them with the respect and kindness that everyone deserves.

School Daze

You spend most of your time in school, so that's probably the place where you'll be putting most of your etiquette skills to work. Naturally, you want to know how to deal with your friends and classmates. But what about your teachers?

Teachers? you say. Are we saying you actually have to be polite to your teachers? You'd better believe it. And if you stop to think about it, it makes sense. Wouldn't school be more pleasant if you knew how to deal with your teachers?

There are rules for proper behavior in the classroom, for both students and teachers. Most teachers are fairly easy to get along with, but some teachers believe (wrongly) that the only way to motivate young people is with fear. Although it can be successful in some cases, the long-term result is often that students grow to resent not only the teacher, but the subject matter as well. This chapter should help you deal with all kinds of teachers, as well as other issues of classroom courtesy.

MISTAKEN CORRECTIONS

Vanessa had a teacher who was constantly making mistakes. Sometimes she would misspell words on the blackboard, and sometimes she said things in class that were just plain inaccurate. A few times Vanessa corrected the teacher in class, and got the distinct feeling that her teacher did not appreciate her comments. On her next report card, the teacher wrote that Vanessa had an "attitude" problem. Vanessa was dismayed; she was only trying to be helpful. Aren't teachers supposed to know what they're talking about? Vanessa felt like she was being punished for being smart.

Vanessa meant well, but she took the wrong action. It is very impolite to correct a teacher, particularly in front of the whole class. Vanessa was right about one thing—a teacher *is* supposed to know what he or she is doing. But teachers are human, and they're entitled to mess up once in a while just like everyone else. Telling a teacher in front of the class that she has made a mistake is bad for several reasons. It is very embarrassing to be told that you have made a mistake, and nobody likes to be embarrassed in front of so many people. In addition, if the class believes that their teacher does not know what she is doing, the teacher will not have much control over the class.

What Vanessa should have done was mention the teacher's mistakes to her after class, in private. However, if a teacher continues to make errors that mislead or confuse the students, the principal should be made aware of it. That way, the principal can correct the teacher and everyone saves face.

WORDS FROM A DEVOTED TEACHER

Dear Smart Talk,

I'm sending you this letter because I thought that your readers might want to know how most teachers feel about their students. Those of us who go into teaching and stay in it do so because we really like kids and want to help them. It makes us feel bad when there's a kid we can't reach, or a student who rejects our offers of help and support.

The greatest reward a teacher receives is when students work to the best of their abilities, and use the knowledge they gain in the classroom to grow as individuals.

When we work hard with a student, we don't expect a reward: That's our job. But it would be nice if students said "thank you" sometimes. You wouldn't believe how many students act as though the teacher was some kind of servant, or a robot that has no needs or feelings. A "hello" in the halls or a smile is also appreciated. When a student greets us outside of class, we feel a special connection with that person. If there's one thing I wish students would keep in mind, it's that teachers are people, too!

Mutual respect and consideration will make school a lot more fun.

RESPONSIBILITIES AND EXPECTATIONS

There are some things everybody can do to make all those hours you spend in the classroom as pleasant as possible. Below are two lists: The first outlines what students should do, and the second summarizes what they have the right to expect from teachers. If everyone followed these rules, school would be an absolutely fabulous place!

Students Should:

✪ *Come to class on time.*

✪ *Settle down to work quickly.*

✪ *Pay attention in class, avoid talking and passing notes, etc.*

✪ *Do homework and other projects carefully and hand them in on time.*

✪ *Bring the necessary materials—textbooks, notebooks, pens, etc.—to class.*

✪ *Maintain an orderly notebook.*

✪ *Raise their hand when wishing to participate in a discussion.*

✪ *Cooperate with the teacher.*

- *Treat the teacher with respect.*

- *Try to be cheerful in class.*

- *Enter and leave the class in an orderly way.*

- *Study for a reasonable amount of time each day.*

- *Thank the teacher at least once a term for his/her help and caring.*

Teachers Should:

- *Be prepared for class.*

- *Present the subject in a reasonably interesting manner.*

- *Be respectful of each student and pleasant to the class as a whole.*

- *Recognize when students are working up to the best of their abilities, regardless of how "good" their work is.*

- *Give an appropriate amount of homework.*

- *Give students a reasonable amount of praise in front of the class.*

- *Avoid embarrassing students.*

- *Assist students who need extra help.*

❂ *Give students adequate feedback on their quizzes and tests so they can learn from their mistakes.*

❂ *Be attentive to personal problems that may be affecting a student's performance during class.*

❂ *Watch for signs of trouble, such as unusual changes in the student's behavior, mood, grades, appearance, etc.*

INSIDE AND OUT

There are also some things that make school life (even outside of the classroom) a little more comfortable. You'll find that if you are courteous to your fellow students, and treat the school, its personnel and its property with respect, school will become a happier place. Below is a brief list of school do's and don'ts.

★★★

Classroom DO's

1. DO respect your fellow classmates.

2. DO say "Excuse me" if you need to get past someone in a crowded hallway or on the stairs.

3. DO respect school property. Do not damage or take anything that does not belong to you.

4. DO observe the same table manners in the cafeteria as you would at home.

5. DO ask the teacher's permission first, if you must leave during class.

6. DO observe school rules at all times.

Classroom DON'Ts

1. DON'T distract other students who are trying to concentrate.

2. DON'T monopolize class discussions, or belittle other people's answers.

3. DON'T push or shove in crowded hallways.

4. DON'T run in the hallways.

5. DON'T yell down the hall to someone. If you must get someone's attention, wave, or wait until they come closer before you speak.

6. DON'T make noise in the halls while classes are in session.

★★★

If additional situations come up and you are unsure of how to deal with them, simply remember the politeness rules and stay courteous and you'll be acting exactly right!

Friends and Manners

No matter what age we are, the status of our friendships has a lot to do with how we feel. Think about it: Isn't just sharing a pizza with your friends a wonderful feeling? And there are really few things worse than fighting with your best friend, right? Friends are wonderful and important to have around, and the best way to make friends is to be a good friend yourself. Being a good friend takes tact, sensitivity and thought. How good a friend are you? Take this quiz and find out.

☆☆ WHAT'S YOUR FRIENDSHIP ☆☆
I.Q.?

1. *Your best friend comes to school in an outfit you desperately wanted to buy, but your folks said it was too expensive. You:*

     a. Tell your friend how great it looks on her.
     b. Tell her you think it would look better on you.
     c. Don't say anything.

2. *You were planning to go to a movie with your friend Mary, but Sue, whom you like better, calls you at the last minute and asks you to go with her. You:*

     a. Call Mary and tell her you're sick, and then go with Sue.
     b. Tell Sue you're going with Mary and suggest another time to go with her.
     c. Suggest you all go together.

3. *You and your friend Mindy always celebrate your birthdays together. This year, she tells you that her parents are going to take her to see a play on her birthday, so she can't spend it with you. You:*

     a. Tell her that if she doesn't spend her birthday with you, she can't be your friend anymore.
     b. Tell her it's okay, but secretly be angry about it.

   c. Suggest that the two of you do something the day before or the day after.

4. *You have two friends that like you and hate one another. You're planning a party and you'd like them both to be there, but you're afraid that their fighting will ruin it. You:*

   a. Invite them both and hope for the best.
   b. Invite the one you like best and hope the other person doesn't hear about the party.
   c. Invite them both, but tell them that their constant fighting upsets you, and ask them to try to get along during the party.

5. *A girl in your class had a party and didn't invite you. You:*

   a. Tease her about it, saying you heard she had a really rotten party.
   b. Understand that it's not realistic to think that you'll always be included in everyone's social plans.
   c. Have a party and invite everyone in the class but her.

6. *A friend of yours gave an incorrect answer in class and you laughed. Now she won't talk to you. You:*

   a. Write a note of apology to her, telling her you didn't mean to hurt her feelings and asking her to be friends again.

   b. Just forget about her. If she really was your friend, she wouldn't be so mad!

   c. Make fun of her in class.

7. *A week ago, you lent your friend some money, but so far she hasn't paid you back. You:*

   a. Decide to write it off as a bad debt.

   b. Politely remind her that she hasn't paid you back.

   c. Send her a bill, with interest.

Answers: Give yourself one point for every right answer: 1) a; 2) b; 3) c; 4) c; 5) b; 6) a; 7) b. *Scoring:* 6–7 correct: Super Friend; 3–5 correct: Good Friend; Less than 3 correct: Friendship Alert! Read this chapter carefully!

☆☆☆

JOUSTING WITH JEALOUSY

Being a good friend means caring and sharing. It means being ready and willing to help others. And above all, it means being understanding, even when your friend does something that drives you crazy!

One of the biggest problems friends face is the "Big Green Monster"—jealousy. It can be jealousy over a boy, over friendship with another girl, over clothes, grades . . . almost anything! It's normal to occasionally feel a little jealous about some things, but if that feeling makes trouble between you and your friends, that's bad news.

Jenny and Alice used to be good friends, but that seems to be all over now. Over the summer, Alice lost a lot of weight, got a flattering new haircut and bought some super clothes. Alice thought Jenny would be just as pleased with her new look as she was herself, but instead, Jenny started making fun of her and calling her "chicken legs." Alice was so hurt that she stopped hanging around with Jenny. But she missed having Jenny for a friend.

Alice was learning a difficult lesson: Sometimes jealousy can really mess up a friendship. Because Jenny feels jealous, she teases Alice. In a way, she might not be able to help herself—jealousy can be a tough emotion to control. What Alice needs to do is to let Jenny know that she's still the same person underneath. Just because she *looks* different doesn't mean she's changed deep down. She should try to understand what Jenny is feeling, and call her and tell her she still wants to be her friend. If Jenny is really a good friend, she'll want to make up.

Keep in mind that showing off is never good manners and can make other people jealous. So don't announce all your A's or wear expensive clothes or jewelry to school. Understatement definitely shows better manners.

SHARE ALIKE

Really close friends share lots of stuff: sodas, secrets and even clothes. This can be a lot of fun, but it can also be a problem. What if you don't feel like telling someone something private, or letting them wear your favorite watch? Can you turn them down without hurting their feelings? And what if all of a sudden your best friend says you can't borrow her new shoes anymore—what do you say?

Maria and Sharon found themselves in a situation like this. They shared absolutely everything with each other! But then, Maria got a gorgeous new sweater for her birthday and Sharon immediately asked if she could borrow it the following night for a date with a boy she really liked. Maria knew Sharon wanted to look her best, and she didn't want to hurt her feelings, but she didn't really want to lend her the sweater that she hadn't even worn herself!

Honesty is the best policy in this case. Maria should tell Sharon how she feels. If Sharon is really her best friend, she will understand. She may not be happy about it at first, but Maria is in the right in this case, and Sharon will realize that at some point.

If Maria wants to be a really super friend though, she'll offer to lend Sharon something else instead—a different sweater, a pretty scarf or maybe a piece of jewelry.

IT'S A SECRET

Sharing secrets can be just as tricky. Linda and Judy told each other absolutely everything! One day, Linda told Judy about how she had a huge crush on a boy named Tom in their science class. They laughed about it and Linda was happy to share this secret with her friend.

But the next day at school, one of Tom's friends came up to her and said, "So, I heard you're in love with Tom. When are you two getting married?" Linda was so mortified she wanted to die. To make it worse, even after thinking about it, Linda was sure that the *only* way anyone could have known about her crush on Tom was if Judy had told them. For the rest of the day, Linda went out of her way to ignore Judy. Judy kept asking her what was wrong, and Linda would say, "You ought to know!"

Secrets lead to mistrust and misunderstandings—so think before you whisper.

Now Linda is miserable. She's lost her best friend, and she's so embarrassed about Tom that she's afraid to go back to school!

Both Linda and Judy are in the wrong in this situation. Of course, Judy should never have told Linda's secret—that's a betrayal of trust. But once the secret was out, Linda behaved badly as well. Instead of ignoring Judy, she should have confronted her friend and asked her if she had told. If Judy had let out the secret, Linda had a right to know why. Maybe Judy didn't realize that it was a secret in the first place. Or maybe she felt that by telling Tom's friend, she might be helping to get Tom interested in Linda.

Misunderstandings will happen, and they're definitely not worth ending a friendship over. Linda might be embarrassed, but the whole thing is sure to blow over in a few days. Tom might even be flattered that Linda likes him! Of course, if Judy deliberately told, Linda has a right to be disappointed. She and Judy can still be friends, but Linda should remember that she can't trust Judy with a secret.

GOSSIP AND RUMORS

Gossip may be fun, but it is definitely bad manners. Even the most "harmless" gossip can come back to haunt you. That's because things can be misinterpreted by different people. What you meant as a compliment could be taken as an insult by someone else. And no matter how hard you try, once something is said, it can't be taken back.

Gossip can also be turned into rumor. Remember playing "telephone" when you were younger? Someone whispered something in another person's ear, and that person passed it on to the next person, and so on down the line until the last person said it aloud. Usually what was said by the last person was nothing like what the first person whispered! Rumors work *exactly* the same way—except that rumors can hurt other people. And often, as a rumor gets passed on it gets exaggerated until it doesn't have any basis in fact anymore!

In general, try to remember to think before you speak. Before you say something, ask yourself the following questions:

✪ *Is this something I want other people to know about?*

✪ *Can I trust this person to keep a secret?*

✪ *Would I be embarrassed if my mother knew this? My teachers? The other kids in school?*

✪ *Is this something that could be misinterpreted or twisted around? What would be the consequences if it were?*

Before you help spread a rumor, ask yourself these questions:

- ✪ *Is the person who told me this reliable?*

- ✪ *Is the person I am talking to trustworthy?*

- ✪ *Would I want someone to say this about me?*

- ✪ *Do I think this story is true?*

- ✪ *What could be the consequences if the wrong people heard this story?*

If you don't like the answers you come up with, don't gossip or spread rumors! It can be entertaining, but it can also hurt, so think about it before you become involved. Not only is it bad manners—but someday you might find you're the one everyone's talking about!

PARTY POWER

Have you ever seen a movie or television show where someone walks into a party and everyone there swoons with delight—this person is so incredibly fun, so confident, so totally cool that no party is complete without him or her?

There are very few party animals around in real life. Most of us even feel a little apprehensive when we go to a party, especially one where we don't know many people. It's just plain awkward to walk into a room and look out over a sea of unfamiliar faces. At some parties, it's tough to fight the impulse to run for the door!

Good manners, though, are designed to make you feel more comfortable at any party. Below are tips from some experienced party-goers that will help you feel much more at ease the next time you go to a party. Check them out!

THE PARTY-GOER'S SURVIVAL GUIDE

You walk into a party and the room is packed with people dancing, talking and having a good time. Everyone seems to be occupied and your host or hostess is nowhere in sight. What do you do?

Smile. Psychologists tell us that facial expressions not only send signals to others, but they can actually change our own feelings! A smile of happiness and confidence, even if you feel like you're only acting, can make you feel more happy and confident.

Relax. If you're stiff and tense, your body language will give you away. If you look relaxed, you will be more approachable and people will be more likely to talk to you.

Look for people you know. If you don't see anyone you know right away, you can always ask someone if they've seen your host or hostess. Besides pointing you in the direction of someone you know at the party, it also gives you the opportunity to ask that person how he or she knows the person who's giving the party. After all, the fact that you're both there means you have something in common.

Get some soda or punch and drink it slowly. This is especially helpful if you feel uncomfortable and don't know what to do with your hands. Getting a drink, and sipping it slowly, gives you something to do. Avoid eating to occupy your hands; if it's a really boring party you could put on a few pounds!

Don't give up on the party after five minutes. Even if you're sure you'll have a terrible time, stick around—sometimes it takes a while for things to warm up.

Don't say anything negative about the party, the host or hostess, the food or the entertainment. No one likes to listen to someone complain, and it's sure to get back to your host or hostess. Besides, if you get the reputation of being a "party critic" you won't get invited to many parties!

You are perfectly justified in leaving a party if you're really uncomfortable for a specific reason (for example, people are drinking or someone has turned out the lights so everyone can make out). Simply find your host or hostess and quietly explain to him or her that you'd like to leave, and thank them for inviting you.

Never leave without telling anyone, no matter how casual a party is. Your friends will worry about you if you disappear suddenly. Also, people might wonder where you are, and that could lead to rumors. Always find your host or hostess first and tell them you're leaving. Thank them and tell them you had a good time. If the party is so crowded that despite your best efforts you can't find your hosts, at least tell someone that you know will see them later to tell them goodbye for you.

Finally, don't forget that in a party situation you should still respect the rules of other people's homes. Parties are not an excuse to be wild or obnoxious.

IT'S MY PARTY

Dear Smart Talk,

A few months ago I moved to Chicago from Milwaukee. I really like living here and I've already made a lot of new friends. Here's the problem: Next month is my birthday and my parents are giving me a big party. It's kind of a combination birthday and housewarming. Some of my friends from Milwaukee are coming and most of my new friends will be there, but there will also be a lot of relatives and friends of my parents and my brother. My parents say that it will be interesting to have so many different groups and generations there, but all I can think of is how I'm going to handle all the introductions! Help!

Susan

Dear Susan,

Never fear! There are rules for introductions, and if you stick to them, you'll find introductions are really quite easy to deal with. Check out the simple guide below:

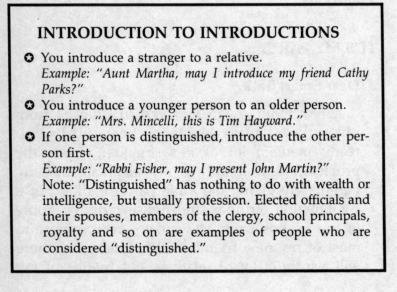

INTRODUCTION TO INTRODUCTIONS

- ✪ You introduce a stranger to a relative.
  Example: "Aunt Martha, may I introduce my friend Cathy Parks?"
- ✪ You introduce a younger person to an older person.
  Example: "Mrs. Mincelli, this is Tim Hayward."
- ✪ If one person is distinguished, introduce the other person first.
  Example: "Rabbi Fisher, may I present John Martin?"
  Note: "Distinguished" has nothing to do with wealth or intelligence, but usually profession. Elected officials and their spouses, members of the clergy, school principals, royalty and so on are examples of people who are considered "distinguished."

All the forms of introduction in the above examples are correct. You can also simply say, "Susan Smith, John Doe" and be just as proper. If you do forget someone's name, you might be able to get away with saying, "This is John Doe." Hopefully, the other person will then introduce himself or herself.

Peer Pressure and the Politeness Puzzle

*D*id you ever feel that your friends were trying to make you do things that you didn't want to do, like smoke cigarettes, or drink wine or beer or even take drugs? That's called "peer pressure," and most people become aware of it in their pre-teen or early teen years. Actually, you've been exposed to peer pressure all your life, but you probably didn't know it! Remember when you felt that you had to have a certain toy because all your friends had it? Or those times you felt that you absolutely couldn't survive unless you wore a certain brand of jeans?

Peer pressure isn't necessarily bad. When people accept the ways of a particular group because they recognize that some kinds of behavior make life better for everyone, that's good. In fact, isn't that part of what manners are about? Well, yes and no. It's important to try to please other people—but never at the expense of your own happiness or safety. And all too often, peer pressure among teens and pre-teens is more destructive than constructive.

Take this quiz and see how you rate on the peer pressure scale.

☆☆   **WHAT'S YOUR PEER**   ☆☆
PRESSURE PROFILE?

1. *Some kids have started to smoke cigarettes in the bathroom at school. They want you to join them. You:*
   a. Know that smoking is bad for your health, so you avoid them while they're doing it.
   b. See that no one appears to be getting sick from it, so you try one puff.
   c. Know that your best friend really wants you to do it too, so you do.

71

2. *You're at a party and everyone is playing kissing games. You don't really like the idea of going into a dark room with a boy, but everyone else is doing it. You:*
   a. Suggest another game that doesn't involve kissing; if they don't like your idea, sit the game out.
   b. Play and go into the room, but then tell the boy that you don't want to kiss him.
   c. Let the boy kiss you and chalk it up to experience.

3. *You see a documentary on television about homelessness, and you want to do something about it in your community. You talk to your friends about it, but they tell you kids can't do anything. You:*
   a. Find an existing group in your community and join it.
   b. Try to convince your friends to start a program to help the homeless.
   c. Decide that your friends are right and resolve to wait until you're an adult to help others.

4. *A boy in your class, whom you think is really neat, tells you he has something he wants you to try. He tells you everyone who's tried it likes it a lot. You realize he's talking about some kind of drug. You:*
   a. Politely but firmly tell him you're not interested.

b. Tell him you'll think about it—it doesn't seem cool to say no right away. Then say no.
c. Try the drug.

5. *Everyone in school is wearing designer jeans with holes torn in them but you. Your parents say they'll give you the money to buy the jeans, but only if you promise not to tear them up. What do you do?*
   a. Start your own fashion trend by wearing untorn jeans with brilliantly colored scarves tied around your waist.
   b. Give up the idea of wearing the jeans completely.
   c. Buy the jeans, tear them up and change into them once you get to school so your parents won't know.

6. *In your crowd, being too smart is considered nerdy. You're a good student, but you want to keep your friends. What do you do?*
   a. Keep up the good work, concentrate on homework and special projects, participate in class, but don't show off.
   b. Do your homework and projects, but don't participate too often in class.
   c. Stop worrying about studying and have fun with your friends. After all, you'll have plenty of work to do when you're older, so why not enjoy the time you have now?

Scoring: The lower your score, the better. Give yourself 1 point for each "a," 2 points for each "b," and 3 points for each "c."

6 points: Great job! Peer pressure doesn't affect you.

7–10: You have a good ability to stand up for your own beliefs. Try thinking more about your options.

11–14: You're flirting with trouble.

15–18: You cave in to peer pressure and that's not good. You'll be happier when you find the courage to do what you know is right!

☆☆☆

Let's consider the answers to the quiz for a moment. What do your answers say about your manners?

Question 1: No matter what, the real question here is your health. It is bad manners for anyone else to ask you to jeopardize it.

Question 2: A is the best answer. But it's important to do this properly. Don't make a scene. Instead, sit quietly in some unnoticeable place, help straighten up or prepare something or excuse yourself to another room. This way you won't disrupt the party, *and* you also save yourself from getting a reputation for being a spoilsport.

Answer B could be a compromise if you really don't want to or can't leave the room. But be careful . . . the boy may think you just don't want to kiss *him*!

Question 3: If your friends are uninterested, then joining an existing group is the best option. Pestering people is impolite and rarely makes them change their minds. It's unrealistic to think that everyone will feel the same way as you do. Just do what you think is best and maybe you'll infect others with your enthusiasm.

Question 4: The *only* correct answer is A. Manners don't count when it comes to drugs.

Question 5: Going along with the crowd against the wishes of your parents is wrong, but don't just sit around and sulk about it either. Sulking is not good manners! Starting your own trend is a good compromise and could really be a fun thing to do, too!

Question 6: A is the best answer. The only thing

you need to be careful about is how you handle yourself around your friends. Do you brag about your grades, or otherwise make it obvious that you're better than your friends at schoolwork? That can hurt them, even if they won't admit it. Keep up with your studies, but keep it low-key.

WHEN TO GET ADULT HELP

If you know that someone is doing something illegal, like taking or selling drugs, stealing or vandalizing, consider telling an adult in authority about it. This can be tough if it means breaking a trust with your friends or if the person doing something illegal seems really dangerous, but there are many good reasons for doing it, too. For one thing, upholding the law is a mature and responsible thing to do. And for another, if you were in trouble in some way, wouldn't you want someone to get help for you?

WITHHOLDING JUDGMENT

Having a group of friends is very important when you're growing up. But what if the group wants you to do something you don't want to do? How can you keep your friends but still be true to yourself?

Marcia found herself faced with this problem. She and her friends started a club called the "Poodles."

They collected stuffed poodles and poodle jewelry, and enjoyed hanging out together. Once a month they had a "Poodle Meeting" where they discussed who they wanted to join their group.

At first the club was a lot of fun. But gradually Marcia began to feel uncomfortable. The group had started out as just a group of friends who had fun together, but then the "Poodle Meetings" turned into gossip sessions about other girls at school. The admissions committee started making all kinds of rules about what type of girl could join—based on things like how attractive the girl was, the clothes she wore and even how well-off her parents were! Some of the girls even started keeping notes on who the other members of the group hung around with at school. If they saw a member with someone they didn't think was good for the group's "image" they brought it up at the meeting and told the girl to drop the "undesirable" friend.

Marcia didn't like this kind of thing, but all her friends belonged to the group and she was afraid they'd never talk to her again if she dropped out of the group. Still, she knew it was wrong to judge people by such superficial standards and she suspected that some of the other girls were just as uncomfortable as she was.

Before the next meeting, Marcia talked to a lot of the girls in private, so she wouldn't be putting them on the spot. Sure enough, many of her friends felt the same way. And at the next Poodle meeting,

Marcia spoke up about the new rules. By then she had the support of the majority of the girls and the Poodles agreed to loosen many of the restrictions.

By being considerate of other people's thoughts and feelings, Marcia was able to reason with her friends without outright criticism of their point of view. Marcia learned an important lesson about peer pressure. You may think that just because "everyone else" does something, it must be right. Of course, that's not true. Strike a healthy balance between what you want and what's considered cool in your crowd. And, if you ever find yourself in a situation where you've got to make a difficult choice, remember that it's easier to say "no" if you can say it nicely.

Dating Etiquette

*O*nce upon a time, the rules of dating were very clear and everyone knew exactly what was expected of them. The boy asked the girl out, he paid, he opened doors for her, helped her into her coat and even ordered her dinner!

Needless to say, modern dating is very different. Girls ask boys out for dates and they often pay for themselves—and for the boy. It's a whole new world, and sometimes the rules are not very clear. What do you know about dating rules today? Take this true/false quiz and see:

☆☆ DATING QUIZ ☆☆

1. *"Dutch Treat" means that you go somewhere with your date and eat Dutch chocolates.*
   True or False

2. *It's okay for the girl to pay for herself on a date.*
   True or False

3. *A boy should always be the one to ask the girl for a first date.*
   True or False

4. *If someone treats you to lunch or dinner, it's okay to order whatever you want, no matter how much it costs.*
   True or False

5. *Even if the boy is paying for the entire date, you should still take money with you.*
   True or False

6. *A curfew is old-fashioned, and has nothing to do with dating today.*
   True or False

7. *Going out in a group can be more fun than going with just one other person.*
   True or False

8. *It's impolite to leave your date if he is being obnoxious. You should stay with him until he brings you home.*
   True or False

9. *If a boy turns down your invitation nicely, you can try again.*
   True or False

10. *Flirting is a good way to get to know someone.*
    True or False

Answers:

1. **False.** Dutch treat means you and the boy split the cost of the date.

2. **True.** It's perfectly okay; you might even want to pay for him, too!

3. **False.** Girls have just as much right to ask.

4. **False.** You don't have to ask him what to order, but you should consider his wallet.

5. **True.** What if he gets lost? Or you want to go home early? Or he loses *his* wallet?

6. **False.** Curfews are often mandatory . . . and sometimes helpful!

7. **True.** Some people think it's for nerds, but they just don't realize how much fun it is to have a bunch of friends around.

8. **False.** You can ask a boy to take you home at any time during the date and, if he refuses, you can leave by yourself.

9. **True.** If at first you don't succeed . . .

10. **True.** And it can be fun, too!

☆☆☆

WHO PAYS?

One of the most delicate things about dating is figuring out who's going to pay without getting into an embarrassing conversation about finances, or worse, an argument. These days, no girl should expect a boy to pay for *everything*. But how do you know when you're expected to pay? Here's a handy guide:

SOLVING THE MONEY PUZZLE

- ✪ If he says, "I'd like to treat you to the movies," he pays.
- ✪ If you say, "I'd like to take you out for a pizza," you pay.
- ✪ If he says, "Let's go to the movies," it's unclear. You might want to suggest going Dutch.
- ✪ If he says, "No, I'd like to pay," you say, "Thank you."
- ✪ In a situation where it is not clear who will be paying, always be prepared to pay for yourself.

Some boys feel that they always have to pay for dates, usually because that's how they've been brought up. With this type of guy, you'll have to make it very clear if you'd like to treat him. But beware—some boys will *never* let you do this, either because they truly believe it's not right, or they're showing off or they think it's not "manly" to let a girl pay. If you date a boy like this, use your best judgment. Don't always suggest expensive outings. For instance, you might suggest renting a video and watching it at your house, or taking a walk in the park.

When it comes to splitting checks, things can get even trickier. Do you split the check right down the middle? Or do you pay for your food and he pays for his? The latter is more fair, but it is definitely not good manners to haggle over a check with anyone, especially on a date. Unless one of you ordered a lot more than the other, it's usually easiest for each to pay half.

Some couples prefer to alternate paying, so that the boy pays for one date and the girl pays for the next. This can work out fine, provided there is a next date, and as long as one of you doesn't always end up paying for the expensive dates.

Another stress-free way to split the cost of a date is to decide who will pay for what. For example, if your date pays for the movie, you can offer to buy the popcorn, or take him out for a slice of pizza afterward. Whether you spend exactly the same amount of money is not the point. Your date will remember that you were thoughtful, and that is the whole idea!

Finally, remember that when a boy pays, you do not *owe* him anything in return: not a kiss goodnight or even another date. In the same way, don't expect a guy to go out with you again just because you paid for your first date. Everyone has the right to say no.

SUCCESSFUL FLIRTING 101

It's fine to know about the etiquette of paying for a date. But what about getting one in the first place? It would be great if you could just go up to someone and say, "I like you," but for some mysterious reason, that's a very hard thing to do. So, a very long time ago, someone invented flirting. Flirting is a nice way of letting someone know that you find him attractive or interesting. But like everything else, there are lots of do's and don'ts. Here's a list to help you survive the flirting game.

★★★

Flirting DO's

1. DO be friendly.

2. DO introduce yourself to the person you like and smile a lot.

3. DO ask questions about the other person.

4. DO compliment the other person on something—doing well on a test, a good answer in class, an article of clothing, etc.

5. DO be sincere.

6. DO show an interest in what the other person says or does.

7. DO be positive.

Flirting DON'Ts

1. DON'T ignore the person you want to attract, hoping this will intrigue him. It won't.

2. DON'T tell other people you like him, hoping

that he'll hear about it. That's embarrassing.

3. DON'T talk about yourself nonstop, hoping to impress him.

4. DON'T say flattering things to him in front of a large group of people, and *don't* grab his hand or put your arm around him. He'll probably feel uncomfortable and he might ignore you completely afterward.

5. DON'T pretend to be someone you're not.

★★★

GETTING TO KNOW YOU

Related to the myth that good manners mean never disagreeing with someone is the idea that you have to listen to whatever anyone says, no matter how boring. Whew! If that's manners, no one could stand being polite! Here's a letter from a girl we know who's having that problem:

Dear Smart Talk:

There's a boy I really like in my class. But whenever I try to talk to him, he acts bored unless I get on the subject of sports. Sometimes we talk about baseball, which I really like, but when he talks about football *I* get so bored I could scream!

86

My best friend told me you should always ask a boy questions about what he's interested in, but that doesn't seem right to me. Am I wrong to expect a boy to talk to me about what interests *me?* Or should I just accept the fact that if I want this boy to like me, I'll have to start watching *Monday Night Football?* Help!

Patricia

Dear Patricia,

There's still a lot of societal pressure for women to cater to men's interests and to consider men's needs above their own. The only way that this will change is if people start to act differently. Begin by talking about what the boy is interested in, so that he'll be comfortable talking to you. Then, gradually introduce other subjects. It may be tough at first, but hang in there! It's worth it.

CONVERSATION CURES

Making conversation is difficult for many people, especially with someone new. And boys can be a mystery! But take heart: They aren't trying to be rude; they're just shy. Because girls mature faster than boys, a lot of boys are less secure socially and have a harder time meeting new people.

Here are some guidelines for making conversation. They don't apply to talking just to boys, though. You can refer to them for talking with a new neighbor, or a relative you haven't seen in a long time or anybody at all! Before long, you'll see how simple it is to get the ball rolling!

First of all, try to find some *common ground*. Even the food in the cafeteria can be a good topic of conversation. Find out whether your new acquaintance is a chili fiend or an egg roll aficionado. Talk about television, movies or books. Nearly everyone has an opinion on these subjects, and you'll each learn about the other's taste.

Talk about things you like to do. For example, if you like horses, say so, and explain why. You might even suggest you go riding together. Who knows? Besides having a more interesting conversation, you might end up with a steady riding partner! But beware: Don't talk someone's ear off about your favorite hobby—they might not find it as interesting as you do!

It is a good tactic to *ask about the other person's interests*. For instance, if you know that someone plays the trumpet, you could talk about music. If his artwork is always being displayed, ask him how long he's been drawing. But don't assume you have to talk about what the other person wants to talk about the whole time. And don't be afraid to change the subject.

There are other things to remember when striking up a conversation. The most important is to *try not to ask "yes or no" questions*—and don't answer a question that way! As we said in Chapter Three, that's the number one reason why some conversations end before they begin. Also, *try not to begin conversations with a negative comment*. Being cheerful and positive is more appealing and will make the other person more interested in talking with you. It's also very difficult to keep a downbeat conversation going—it's too depressing!

Finally, never put down something another person says or disagree merely for the sake of having something to discuss. And if the conversation does get heated, refer to the tips in Chapter Two for arguing gracefully.

ASK AWAY

Some girls are afraid to ask a boy for a date, but that's silly! If you expect a boy to be brave enough to ask you, shouldn't you be brave enough to ask him? It was not always considered feminine for a girl to ask a boy out, but fortunately times have changed. Today, most people feel that it's okay for either person to ask.

There are right and wrong ways to ask for a date,

If your date takes you to the movies, why don't you treat him to popcorn?

however. For one thing, you should always be direct. Say something like, "I have two tickets for a baseball game on Saturday. Would you like to go with me?" Be straightforward and specific. If you beat around the bush, he might not understand what it is you're asking.

Try suggesting a particular activity such as a movie, a baseball game or a party. That way, if he hates baseball, for example, he can suggest something else before it's too late. And have an alternative suggestion in mind, in case the person you ask is busy on the first date you suggest.

Always be friendly and positive. Keep a "smile" in your voice.

Of course there are a few things to *avoid* when asking for a date as well. For instance, don't say, "Are you doing anything Saturday night?" This is incredibly rude because technically the boy doesn't know why you're asking. You've already put him in an awkward situation, and set yourself up to get your feelings hurt.

Don't take "no" as an indication that he never wants to go out with you. Ask him if he'd like to do something another day. And if the answer really is "no," don't be hurt. Just remind yourself that he's missing out on a good time with a terrific girl. Besides, there are plenty of other guys around!

A GIRL'S GUIDE TO DATING

You've finally asked him out, or he's asked you—now what? You may be so worried about what to expect and how to behave that you begin to wish you'd never agreed to go out with him in the first place. Never fear! If you remember to be polite and considerate, you can't go wrong. Here are some things to keep in mind that should make dating a breeze.

Be ready at the appointed time. Don't make him sit and wait for you.

Dress appropriately. You should know where you're going by now. If for some reason there's been a mix-up, don't panic. If he shows up all dressed up and you're in jeans, say, "Oh, Jeff, I didn't realize I should dress up. Would you mind waiting a moment while I change?" Then change *quickly*.

Introduce your date to your family and chat for a minute or two. Don't rush him out of the house as if you're ashamed of him.

Always make sure a parent knows where you're going, in case there's an emergency and they need to get in touch with you. If you're going to someone's house, make sure your parents have the address and phone number.

Make sure you know when you have to be home. This may seem like a drag, but it can work to your advantage as well. Most of the time you'll wish you could spend more time with your date, but once in a while you'll be happy to say, "I have to be home by . . ." Not every date is terrific.

Never make a secret date with someone or give your parents false information about where you'll be. That's just asking for trouble. Anyone who urges you to lie to your parents is someone who is not concerned with your well-being. This is someone you should not be going out with, no matter how terrific he seems.

If your date starts doing something illegal or dangerous, such as drinking or taking drugs, *go home immediately.* Don't worry about hurting his feelings or seeming impolite.

When you first start dating, try going out with a group of people, even if everyone is paired off. That way if things don't go well, you won't have to suffer alone. Having friends around is also a good way to get conversation going so that you and your date can get to know each other in a relaxed setting.

Always say "please" and "thank you" for things during a date and, afterward, thank your date for taking you out. Tell him you had a nice time. It's even okay to say you hope you can do it again sometime. But remember, a first date is not a guarantee of a second. Don't be crushed if he doesn't call you the next day. Relax!

Even if the date was a total disaster, don't bad-mouth the boy or complain about him to other people. Maybe you two just weren't right for each other. Don't give the boy a reputation for being a "bad date." And don't give yourself a reputation for being picky!

Dating can be one of the most exciting parts of your life. It's a terrific feeling to know that you're special to someone. And knowing good dating etiquette—and learning to respect the feelings of your date—will really help you on the road to romance.

The Tough Stuff

*D*o you ever feel like your life is turning into a soap opera called, "My Most Embarrassing Moments?" Life used to be so simple, but these days it seems like everything in the world is out to get you, to make you look as stupid and clumsy as possible. Don't give up! No matter how bad your goof seems now, in a year or two no one will remember what happened. Maybe not even you! And in ten years, whatever it was won't make a bit of difference.

And when things look blackest, don't forget: Something just as bad—or worse—has happened to everyone at some time or another.

COMBAT THE CLUMSIES

Manners can help you deal with these embarrassing situations. Sure, we all experience them—but the better you handle it, the better you'll feel about it afterwards.

Dear Smart Talk,

Most kids know that eating in the school cafeteria can be dangerous to their health. But they don't realize that it can also be dangerous to your pride! The other day I was attacked by a plate of "killer spaghetti." I was about to start on a plate of spaghetti and meatballs when, suddenly, it was all over me! I honestly don't know how it happened: It was like the stuff was alive! And to make it worse, I just couldn't get the mess cleaned up. Everyone in the cafeteria was laughing their head off. I just wanted to die! Luckily I got to go home to change my clothes, but now I feel like I never want to set foot in school again. Help!

Pam

Dear Pam,

It's amazing how differently you feel about food that has landed in your lap and not your mouth! Fortunately this kind of thing doesn't happen too often. But in case it ever happens again, there are ways to minimize the damage to your pride.

Most important: DON'T PANIC! The first thing you should do in an awkward situation is take a deep breath.

Try not to call attention to yourself by jumping up from the table, screaming or bursting into tears. Why play to an even bigger audience? Ask a friend to get some paper towels, and clean up the mess quickly and quietly.

If it's a disaster beyond the paper-towel stage, do the best you can to clean yourself up and then send a friend to find a school custodian. If it's early in the school day, go to the nurse's office and ask to call one of your parents for a fresh set of clothes. But if that's impossible, just hold your head up and try to get through the day as if nothing was unusual. You shouldn't call attention to something that you're uncomfortable about.

Hopefully, the other kids will be understanding and not tease you about it, but if someone has the very bad manners to say something nasty about it, make it into a joke. Say something like, "If you think *I* look bad, you should see the plate of spaghetti!"

Occasionally, accidents may happen in which someone else's property gets damaged. For example, you're eating dinner at a friend's house and you accidentally drop and break an expensive serving dish. If this happens to you, the very first thing you should do is apologize and offer to clean the mess up. But don't insist on helping if your offer is refused.

As soon as you get home, write a note to your friend and his or her parents thanking them for having you to dinner. Apologize for breaking the dish and offer to pay for the broken item. And the next time you're invited to their house (yes, there will be a next time) be extra-careful when you're helping to clear the table.

ONE ON ONE

Sometimes you can embarrass yourself, not in front of a lot of people, but in front of one person. But if the person is someone you're trying to impress, it can seem about ten times worse! This is what happened to Jessica. . . .

Jessica was riding her bike toward the house of a boy she really liked. She was daydreaming, wondering if he would be outside. If he were, would he wave? She was wearing a terrific new shorts set, just in case. As she approached Jason's house, she saw him—and he waved! As she lifted her hand to wave back, her tire hit a crack in the sidewalk and she went flying over the handlebars right onto his lawn! Although she wasn't injured, Jessica wished she were dead.

Her first impulse was to run away, but she knew that would make her look even more ridiculous— besides being rude. Instead, she realized she would have to make the best of it. Fortunately for her, Jason had run up to see if she was okay. When she realized he wasn't laughing at her, she felt better immediately. He invited her into the house for a glass of water and, before Jessica knew it, they were talking and laughing like old friends. Before Jessica left, they had made a date to go bike riding together that weekend. And all because Jessica didn't lose her head—except over Jason, that is.

IT WAS HERE A MINUTE AGO

Sometimes an embarrassing situation is caused by thoughtlessness—or forgetfulness. It can be something as simple as forgetting that a party is semiformal and showing up in shorts, or arriving at a birthday party and realizing that you've left the guest of honor's present at home.

Careful planning can lessen the chances of this happening, and if you're forgetful you should make a point of being absolutely sure you've got everything before you leave the house. Try making check lists for yourself. Nothing will ever guarantee that you'll never forget anything, however. The good news is that there are ways to turn these embarrassing situations into triumphs of ingenuity. Here's a letter from a very bright girl:

Dear Smart Talk:

Recently I invited my best friend out for ice cream to celebrate the end of the school year. She really pulled me through history class! As I was getting ready to leave the house to meet her, my brother hit me up for an emergency loan. Since I had a little extra money, I took out my wallet and gave the money to him. A little while later I went out to meet my friend.

After we finished our ice cream, I asked for the check and reached into my purse for my wallet.

That's when I realized that I hadn't put it back again after giving my brother the money. I meant to, but I was in a hurry and I just forgot! I had visions of Janet and myself washing dishes forever!

Keeping a list will help keep you on track.

Then, all of a sudden, I remembered that the manager of the ice cream parlor is a friend of my parents'. I explained to him what had happened and he told me I could bring him the money later, which I did. I was really lucky, but what if I hadn't known the manager?

Serina

Dear Serina,

Your quick thinking saved the day. You did the right thing and saved yourself from embarrassment. More important, you remained calm, which allowed you to think clearly.

If this ever happens in a restaurant where you don't know anyone, however, play it cool. Excuse yourself, then go to see the manager and explain what has happened. Show some ID (you should always carry something in your pocket: a school ID, or something else with your name and picture on it). Ask to call your parents. They may be able to pay with their credit card over the phone. If this isn't possible, ask your parents to talk to the manager and see if it would be okay to send the restaurant a check. Most of the time this is perfectly acceptable.

No matter how embarrassing the situation, good manners and quick thinking make it much easier to cope with. Someday, you'll probably even be able to laugh about it.

Good Manners
Wherever You Go

Y ou've seen how manners can help you through the day-to-day disasters and puzzlements of growing up. But you may be wondering what became of all the little courtesies you probably associate with "real" manners. That's what this chapter is all about. There are certain rules of etiquette for certain specific places and situations, and the following tips should serve as a guide on how to behave anywhere you go.

EVERYDAY TRIPS

If you're going downtown by bus, train or subway, the rules are simple: Just remember to be considerate of the other passengers at all times. This means refraining from pushing or shoving, no matter how crowded the car is. If you *must* push past someone to get out, remember to say "Excuse me." (There's certainly no point in missing your stop simply to be polite to someone in your way!) If possible, don't stand in front of the door unless you're getting out at the very next stop.

When entering the bus, train or subway, stand aside first to let the arriving passengers out. (This rule applies to elevators as well.) Once on board, refrain from activities that may be annoying to the other passengers, such as playing a radio, talking very loud or yelling across the aisles. Eating and

It's important to be polite wherever you go, even on the subway or bus!

drinking on board should also be avoided. You may think that your soda could not possibly inconvenience anyone. But just think about what might happen if the train or bus suddenly stopped short! Besides, food and drink are usually not allowed on public transportation and you should observe the rules of the bus or subway at all times. They're there to assure your safety and comfort and that of the other passengers.

Then there is the age-old question of who should give up his or her seat to whom. It used to be that men gave up their seats to women (of any age) and elderly men while young women gave up their seats to older people. These days, the safest rule of thumb is to consider a standee's physical condition as well as the number of bundles he or she is carrying.

An obviously pregnant woman (be careful about this one!) should be offered a seat, as should anyone on crutches or using a cane. You may also offer your seat to an elderly person, someone carrying a baby or someone with an armful of packages. If the person refuses and you think they're just being polite, you may offer one more time, but don't persist! Don't be insulted if they refuse—or if they're insulted that you asked. When you're not sure whether to give up your seat, it's probably better to err on the side of good manners and offer it.

What if someone offers you his seat? Unless you're loaded up with packages or you're not feeling well, simply smile and say "No, thank you."

LONGER TRIPS

The rules for a train or plane are generally the same as those for a bus or subway, except that you sometimes have a reserved seat on a long train trip, and you nearly always have one on a plane. Again, be considerate of the other passengers. Don't cause a commotion by jumping in and out of your seat, especially if you're not on the aisle. Don't hog the seat next to you by placing your coat, purse, packages and so forth on it, especially if the plane or train is crowded. Make sure you check any oversized baggage (this is for safety as well as convenience). Food is allowed on flights—usually the airline will provide free soft drinks and peanuts, with a meal or snack on longer flights. It is also perfectly okay to bring your own food, as long as it is not too messy. The same goes for trains.

Be sure to dispose of your trash properly when you leave. On a plane the flight attendants usually collect it; but on a train it's up to you! Trains are not cleaned as often as planes are, so be considerate of the passengers who will ride after you.

VISITING

When visiting someone else's house, you should always observe the rules of the home in which you are a guest. Different families have different routines, and you should not disrupt them just because that isn't the way things are done at your house. The fact that you are not a member of that family is no excuse.

Has this ever happened to you? While having dinner at a new friend's house, Linda was trying to be on her best behavior—and then something unexpected happened. After everyone was served, Linda was picking up her fork to take a bite when she realized that her friend's family had their heads bowed in prayer. Linda was taken aback. Her family never said grace and she didn't know how to react, so she just put down her fork and bowed her head respectfully.

This is exactly the right thing to do. You certainly don't have to pray, but you should be polite to the family. You can be sure that your friend's family is doing it because it is an important tradition in their household, and it is only polite to respect their traditions.

Never use something that belongs to your hosts without asking first. This includes helping yourself to food and drink and especially using the telephone! Even if you are making a local call, clear it with your friend or his or her parents first. If for some reason you need to make a long-distance call—for example, if you are staying with a friend who lives out of town and you have to call your folks about travel arrangements or something important like that—you should call collect (or use your family's telephone credit card number).

Finally, treat everyone in the household with respect, not only your friend. Address his or her parents as Mr. and Mrs. So-and-so, and continue to call them that unless they specifically ask you to call them something else. And even if your friend and her brother are fighting all the time and he's a Class-A creep, you have to be nice to him, too.

SPECIAL RULES FOR OVERNIGHT STAYS

Sleep-overs are probably a pretty popular pastime among you and your friends, and they can be a whole lot of fun. However, there are a few things you should remember:

Always bring everything you need. If it's a slumber party with several girls, this may include towels, a sleeping bag and pillows. If it isn't clear what you're supposed to bring, check with your friend first.

If you'll be staying with a family for several days, it's considered polite to bring them a gift, which needn't be expensive. One nice idea, especially if your hosts live far away, is to bring them something unique to your part of the world. For example, a New Englander might bring a bottle of maple syrup.

Keep the area assigned to you neat. This means making your bed each day and not throwing your clothes all over the floor. You are not in a hotel and shouldn't expect maid service! The same goes for the bathroom—hang up your wet towels and put the cap on the toothpaste.

Don't forget to thank your host and hostess when you leave, and be sure to send a thank-you note.

TRAVELING ABROAD

If you have the opportunity to travel, you're lucky! Think of all the sights you'll see, the foods you'll eat, the different customs . . .

Wait a minute! Did we say different customs? Yes, it's true. Even within the United States, customs can vary from place to place. But especially in other countries, it's important to respect the customs and ideas of any place you visit.

When you're in another place, you may feel a little uncomfortable at first. People may speak a different language, or do things differently. But one of the joys of travel is to have new experiences. Don't fight them! If you try to "fit in" you'll enjoy yourself more. On the other hand, if you spend all your time looking for things that are "just like home" you'll be frustrated and find yourself wondering what's so great about the place you're visiting. This is a waste of a good vacation!

Don't be rude or offensive to the natives of the

country you're visiting. Especially, don't be insulted if they don't speak English! It's true that many foreigners learn English in school, but remember, in another country *you're* the foreigner. So, try to learn a few basic words and phrases in the language they speak.

Bon voyage!

EATING OUT

Eating in a restaurant is a lot like eating at home—except that you have to pay. Otherwise, if you have good table manners at home, you shouldn't have any trouble when dining out. There are a few minor differences, though, that you ought to know about.

First, be considerate of your fellow diners, especially in a restaurant that is crowded or where the tables are close together. Don't talk at the top of your lungs, sing ("Happy Birthday" is the only exception) or eavesdrop on the other customers.

Second, don't be rude to your waiter. He or she is not your slave. You should expect decent treatment in return, however. Your order should be taken promptly and your meal served promptly, cooked as you requested. If it is not—for instance, if your "rare" steak is burned black—you may send it back.

Don't make a scene, just point out the problem to the waiter. If he or she gives you a hard time, calmly ask to speak to the manager. Asking for a doggie bag is also perfectly acceptable.

WHAT ABOUT TIPPING?

You should usually leave a fifteen percent tip. If the service is particularly good, leave up to twenty; if the service was absolutely terrible, feel free to leave a good deal less. Some people believe that it is okay to leave no tip if the service was bad. No one can tell you what to do, but don't forget that the tip is usually a good part of the waiter or waitress' salary. Also, always ask yourself whether bad service was entirely the waiter or waitress' fault.

TIPPING ELSEWHERE

Hairdressers should be tipped about fifteen percent, unless the person who does your hair is the owner of the salon, in which case you should *not* tip him or her. The person who shampoos your hair also gets a small tip—a dollar is fine.

Cab drivers expect a fifteen to twenty percent tip.

Sometimes you may find yourself in a place that has a ladies' room attendant. Here, use your judgment. If all she does is hand you a towel, some change should be enough. But if you use any of the makeup, hair spray, sewing materials, etc. that she provides, you should tip fifty cents or more, depending on the amount of service.

SHOPPING SOLUTIONS

For some reason, people seem to think that because they're spending money in a store they have the right to behave as rudely as they wish. This is not true! You should always be courteous in a store, to the other shoppers and to the salespeople.

Don't toss clothes on the floor of the dressing room, or pull them off the rack and leave them on the floor, or put them on another rack. Try to put them back neatly where you found them, or give them to a salesperson or the fitting room attendant, if there is one.

Don't push or shove in a crowded store, or stand in front of an entire rack of clothes for ages so that no one else can see it.

Treat the salesperson like the human being he or she is. Smile and be polite. Wait patiently if the line at the counter is long. You are perfectly justified in complaining, however, if the salesperson is missing or is talking on the phone instead of helping customers.

GIFT GIVING—AND RECEIVING

Few things bring as much pleasure as receiving a wonderful gift, but choosing the perfect gift for someone else can actually come pretty close. When it comes to gift giving, there are just a few things to keep in mind.

Choose something you're reasonably sure the receiver will appreciate. Don't give your nonsmoking uncle an ashtray, for example, and don't give a box of chocolates to a friend who is trying to lose weight.

Remember to take the price tag off the gift. It's really tacky to let someone know what you paid for something. You should keep the receipt, though, in case the gift is damaged or for some other reason needs to be returned.

Don't buy someone a present that is obviously a good deal more expensive than the gift they gave you for a similar occasion. Even if your intentions are good, the person's feelings may be hurt, or they may think you're showing off. Similarly, when receiving a wonderful gift, never cry out, "Wow! I bet this cost a fortune!"

Courtesy is knowing how to give—and how to receive!

Always remember to write thank-you notes immediately for any gifts you receive. If someone neglects to write you a thank-you note, don't point it out to them. It's bad manners to notice someone else's bad manners. But if there is really an honest doubt in your mind as to whether the person received the present, you can ask him or her.

Happily Ever After

Manners are not just old-fashioned ideas or rules someone invented to embarrass people who don't know them. You use them every day, often without even realizing it. As you've seen throughout this book, manners can really make life much easier—for everyone.

No book can give you the answer to every problem, however. If you find yourself in a potentially embarrassing situation and you don't know what to do, don't panic. Think about the ten puzzle pieces from Chapter One, and decide which one best fits the situation. Common sense will do the rest.

And remember: Being caring and considerate and using common sense are what manners are all about. So, just let the real, beautiful you shine through, and you'll go through life being a very courteous and absolutely wonderful person!

SMART TALK Has It All!

Some of the best tips for fashion, fun and friendship are in the Smart Talk series. Learn how to look and feel your greatest, create your own personal style, and show the world the great new you! Smart Talk points the way:

Skin Deep
Looking Good
Eating Pretty
Feeling Fit
Finishing Touches—Manners with Style
Now You're Talking—Winning with Words
Dream Rooms—Decorating with Flair
Great Parties—How to Plan Them
How to Make (and Keep) Friends